THE MAKING OF AN ENTREPRENEUR

Giving Birth to the Entrepreneur in You

Erika T. Moore

www.meppublishing.com

www.erikatmoore.com

www.gettingpaidwitherika.com

This book is designed to provide accurate and authoritative information with regard to the subject matter covered. This information is given with the understanding that neither the author nor MEP Publishing is engaged in rendering legal, professional advice. Since the details of your situation are fact-dependent, you should additionally seek the services of a competent professional.

The opinions expressed by the author are not necessarily those of MEP Publishing.

Published by MEP Publishing.

210 Riverview PL | Lillington, North Carolina USA

1.910.814.1554 | www.meppublishing.com

MEP Publishing is committed to excellence in the publishing industry. The company reflects the philosophy established by the founders, based on Habakkuk 2:2 *"And the LORD answered me, and said, Write the Vision, and make it plain upon tables, that he may run that readeth it..."*

Published in the United States of America

ACKNOWLEDGMENTS

First and foremost, giving honor and praise To My LORD and Savior, JESUS CHRIST who is the head of my life and the center of my joy. In him, I live, move, and have my total being. I like to thank my church family, Praise God International Ministries for loving and supporting me in all of my endeavors. I make sure I absorb every nugget of wisdom you bestow upon me. I have now taken full accountability and responsibility for my economy and I stand on Deuteronomy 8:18. I would like to thank my publishing company MEP Publishing for all the work you do behind the scenes that keep my work equitable. To my business partners and family all over the United States, thank you for being such a great support system and inspiration. To my Sister's With Purpose groups, and my women ministry, you all keep me focused and living up to my full potential. To my beloved husband Adolph; who is truly the best entrepreneur I know. I love you. Thank you for not allowing me to quit. Thank you for being a living example of what hard work and persistence look like. Because of your Godly example, I can awaken five in the morning and begin working and writing like a champion.

ABOUT THE AUTHOR

Erika T. Moore was born Erika Tracey Williams on September 5, 1969, to Sandra Williams and Roland Nowell. She was born and raised in Wyandanch, New York. She was raised with two sisters and two brothers. Erika always enjoyed writing ever since she was a little girl in elementary school. She graduated from Wyandanch Memorial High School in June 1987.

Erika is the pastor of Praise God International Ministries in Lillington NC, alongside her husband Apostle Adolph Moore. She is a retired Educator from Wyandanch Union Free School district. She enjoys writing, reading good novels, and educational and business literature. She also enjoys singing and writing music as well as cooking and baking.

TABLE OF CONTENTS

INTRODUCTION

Ever since I was a little girl I can recall my love for writing. It became a part of my lifestyle, even when I wasn't operating and functioning in my gifts. I will write things down unnecessarily, just so I can satisfy my urge of writing. Writing has always made me feel big and powerful.

The sole purpose of designing this course and writing another terrific book is because if you are anything like me, you are probably either a late bloomer with your entrepreneurial gifts or perhaps, you don't know what you desire to do or even know how to get started. I was once all of these at the same time.

I knew I loved writing, but how do I advance in the world of literature with no degree? So because of this, I paralyzed myself and my gifts and I will spend decades drifting to and fro and never being satisfied with myself. I will write countless novels but will do nothing with them and they too will drift away. I was forced to recognize my gifts when being pushed into the role of an entrepreneur when I was injured on my job on November 7, 2014.

This book is designed to help you recognize your gifts and role as an entrepreneur and to step into your gifts by choice instead of being pushed. I remember growing up, and going to our community pool and the kids would yell" come on in Erika". What are you waiting for? Truth is, I wasn't ready. And all of a sudden fear was overtaking me, while I helplessly, being engulfed by the coldness of the water. See what had happened was the kids were tired of my excuses and someone was pushing me into the water. The problem was, I never learned how to swim. Now I enjoyed the water with my non-swimming self. And I admit I had fun once I got over the initial fear.

Many of us are pushed into our God-given roles of being business owners and doing what we love and enjoy doing. The truth is after the initial push, fear we once faced is now just a vivid memory. Then you began to say things like this, I should have done this a long time ago, or what was I afraid of?

In this book, we will help some develop their God-given talents and others to help recognize it. Once we break down the walls you have willingly built to prevent you from winning, then we will show you how to build your new foundation and you will begin living the life you were designed to live. In the book of Habakkuk 2:1&2, it says, v1- I will stand upon my watch, and set me upon the tower, and will watch to see what he will say unto me, and what I shall answer when I am reproved. V2- And the LORD answered me, and said, Write the vision, and make it plain upon tables, that he may run that readeth it.

WINTER

"A period like a winter, as the last or final period of life; a period of decline, decay, inertia, dreariness, or adversity."

Thesaurus.com

CHAPTER 1

GOING THROUGH THE SEASONS

Proverbs 20:4 The sluggard will not plow because of the cold; *therefore* shall he beg in harvest, and *have* nothing.

Seasons are an essential part of life here on Earth. Each function of seasons affects the weather, growth, agriculture, but they also have a strong impact and affect humanity in the way we think, live and our total being. Have you ever heard that someone acts funny during certain times of the year? Well, it's true and it's equated to the different seasons we are in.

Ever since I was a little girl growing up in Long Island, New York. I have always disliked the colder months of the year, which are December, January, February, and partially the month of March. I will dread leaving the warmth and comfort of my home to fight the brutal and wicked cold weather.

In my research, I find it's easier for people to equate their bad attitudes and strong dislikes for the coldness to the winter seasons. I concur, only because I wasn't as happy and friendly as I usually am. I've allowed the cold weather to dictate my ability to persevere. I blame this due to lack of discipline and consistency, I became enslaved to this season instead of prosperous.

As I write this, I am reminded of something Steve Harvey shared with his listeners. He gave an analogy of a flea. He said (and of course I am paraphrasing) the flea is born with a 36 degree vertical. This allows the flea the ability to jump extremely high. However; if the flea is caught and placed into a mid-size jar he will not be able to jump as high.

The purpose being is because it adapted to its environment. And if you fill the jar with more fleas, eventually they will all have the same fate and now, they will mate with each other to produce more fleas. And in their new environment, their baby fleas will never know that they were created to have 36 degrees vertical because they will only replicate what they see.

Many of us are replicating what we have witnessed our parents and grandparents and great grandparents have shown us. We manage to do just enough to stay afloat. Many of our dreams and passions are just a vivid thought of our imagination. You will never bring it to life because it's never been done before in your family genealogy and because of lack of faith, it'll be submerged and buried alive in your subconscious.

To be relentless, you must be willing to go against the odds and challenges that you will be faced with. Stop falling prey to your environment and learn how to pray to change your environment. God created you with greatness in mind. He created you to stand out from the rest. Stop allowing people with no dreams, goals, passions, and hunger to be great to steal your passion. Stop allowing fearful people to counsel and guide you.

How can someone living paycheck to paycheck with no solution to their immediate situation talk to you about financial freedom, wealth, and success?

How can someone with no thrive, motivation, and determination advise you, on what you should be doing regarding your life?

God-given you, your gifts. Why have you not opened it? Better yet, why are you not grateful and utilizing it? Why do you accept being different as being a crime? What has mediocracy done for you? What is duplicating what others have and are doing, working for you?

You were created to be different from your community and environment. You were born to be great.

Stay away from people who have never owned anything but owe everybody such as, homes, cars, businesses. These people are hazardous to your health and wealth.

To be relentless, you must first have a vision, goals, and a sound plan. Begin to write your vision down and read it to yourself aloud at least twice a day. It makes no sense to write it and don't read it. You must become intentional.

You must now act, move, and strategically plan on purpose. You must speak things into existence as if they are already done. Greet yourself as the King and Queen you are. Speak life and walk Faith. This is the season of being INTENTIONAL.

Instead of focusing on the things you dislike about the winter season. Recondition your mind to concentrate on building and creating great things this season. Dream BIG, Want BIG, and Go BIG! This is the season when entrepreneurs go extremely hard to bring their; passions to life.

Many people have the same issues that I once possessed during the winter seasons. I dare you now to begin to observe the attitudes and mindsets of your colleagues, employer, family, spouse, children, and friends during this season. Perhaps this may be you. Examine yourself during each season and begin to modify your behavior accordingly.

As I began to recognize the gifts I possessed, I began to examine and modify my behavior. I immediately noticed that I will work less during the colder seasons and complain more. Was this an even exchange in the environment? These are questions that I've been forced to ask myself honestly. As I listened to one of my coaches, Dr. Eric Thomas, (I claim him to be my coach because I listen to his inspirational and empowering motivational speeches every morning) said that we must begin to confront the "Me' in me. He went on to say, (and of course I am paraphrasing) we get mad at everyone who disappoints us but give ourselves passes when we mess up.

He was correct. I blamed everyone for their shortcomings but constantly overlooked my very own. How hypocritical is that?

To walk and grow into your full Godly potential, you must recognize and acknowledge your shortcomings as well as your strengths.

In the space below identify your weaknesses and strengths:

My Weaknesses are:

- _____
- _____
- _____

My Strengths are:

- _____
- _____
- _____

In the exercise below, ask yourself if your weaknesses affect you in the winter seasons, if yes explain why?

How do you perform overall in the winter seasons?

What Kind Of Worker Are You?

Are you an Ant or Are you a Bear?

Now that you have identified your strengths and weaknesses; it's now time to move towards your work ethics in winter. In the following section, we learn that our mood has a strong impact on how we live on a day to day basis. In my research, I have discovered that during daylight savings time, when we have more daylight, people are more active and more productive. The human body has adapted to the concept that you can get more done when it's daytime. Have you ever heard someone say, let's get an early start so we can make the best of the day? Why do you think so many people believe this concept? It has a lot to do with being able to see more during the daytime. It's even less cold during the daytime.

But when nightfall, we embark on a whole new territory. Most people are afraid of the darkness; some equate darkness with colder temperatures. Many people have visual problems and it becomes harder to see or to get any work done. Now I do understand that there are people who are opposite of the seasons.

Why Do Bears Hibernate?

The sole purpose of hibernation for bears is because they do tend to slow down during the colder months. Does this sound familiar? Even though they do go into a deep sleep, they are not solely in hibernation. The Black, Brown, and Grizzly bears are known as torpor bears and they hibernate to escape the cold.

Also during the cold seasons, their food supply is scarce. The bear is different from the ant and I will go further into the ant, later on in the book. The bear understands that their survival rate will not be strong in the colder months, so it's easier for them to lay low, regain their strengths, and come back stronger in the warmer seasons.

What I find fascinating about hibernation is that the bears do not need food to survive, nor do they eat, urinate and defecate during hibernation. If you are anything like me, you're probably asking how is this possible? I learned that bears live off of a layer of fat that was built up during the summer and fall seasons before them going into hibernation.

Their waste products are produced. Instead of releasing it, it's recycled.

Many of us are like bears during hibernation. Instead of working harder and developing our gifts and talents that are produced within us. Instead of releasing it, we recycle our gifts. What good is a present that you never give to the person it was intended for?

Many reading this book are great inventors, writers, athletes but no one will ever know, all due to you keeping your natural-born talent bottled up inside. God said he will withhold no good thing from us. So my question is then why are you withholding your gifts not only from the world but from you? It's not the time to slow or shut down during your unfavorable season. It's time to really ignite yourself and go forth. Don't stop now, there's purpose in your winter season. Many great things occur during these seasons that are both beneficial to the earth and humanity.

Ask yourself, what are your principles? Began to set high standards, feed the hunger you possess, and develop a strong desire for urgency. Even though it's never too late to start; however; you have wasted valuable time. The time you will never see again nor will you get it back. Take advantage of your "Now" while you are eager and willing to put the effort forth.

Please know that it's impossible for everything to be done in one day. This is why it's important to create goals, so you can begin doing little by little day by day. The key is doing something daily.

I'm reminded of one of my favorite quotes from Dr. Les Brown, he says: "When change comes, opportunity begins". Be willing to accept the changes in your life while embracing the opportunities that are being presented to you.

Failure is success. Ponder on this. Had it not been for your failures, you would have never known how determined, resilient, and successful you are. Every millionaire built their success on past failures.

Farmers and agriculturists all plant their crops in the warmer weather so they can reap a great harvest, so come the colder seasons, they will not lack in any area. Why are you stopping? It's time to reevaluate your concept and mindset towards your weaker season (your personal weaknesses) and develop a plan that you will begin to prosper even when you're not in your season of favor.

This is the season to tap into personal development and growth. This is the season for you to "GET BETTER". Things don't get better by you thinking that they are. Things get better when you get better.

Jim Rohn is one of my favorite motivational speakers. His words of wisdom and knowledge have allowed me a better outlook on life and my personal endeavors. I'm reminded of one of his messages about the seasons.

Through his teaching, his message was for us to "learn how to handle (your) seasons better". He encourages us to become wiser, stronger, and better during our seasons.

If winter is the season you do not like, then learn how to handle this season instead of this season handling you. Now is the time to adhere to wise instructions for your life. "Hear instructions, and be wise, and refuse it no"t. Proverbs 8:33

Ask yourself how your entrepreneurial performance did, during these past 12 winters? Did you incline in your passion or was there a great decline?

What is it about the calendar winter seasons that allow you not to strive towards your full potential?

Jim Rohn goes on to explain the various kinds of winters, which I'll do my best to paraphrase for you.

The first winter he refers to is the "winter when you seem to can't figure things out':

- Whether it's pertaining to a life decision such as employment,
- Relationships, marriage, engagement, divorce
- Life decisions

- Relocation
- Hair color/hairstyle
- Buying a new car
- Starting your own business
- Finances

These are some of the things that fall under this category.

Another catastrophic category for this season is: "The winter when it all goes wrong

- Loss of employment/wages
- Divorce/break up
- Children not listening
- Unable to meet financial obligations
- Business closes down
- Death

These are just a few things for this season

The next category is "The winter of your life"

- Social winters,
- Political winters(worldwide)
- Economical winters

There is more to winter than the cold season and Christmas.

The solution for getting through this difficult season for you is; accepting this major season for being a part of your life and simply getting better at handling this unfavorable season. No matter how much you try to avoid it, it's never going away and is guaranteed to come when it's the appointed time of the year. You cannot prevent or change it from coming, but you surely can change yourself and how you utilize this season to benefit your personal development and growth.

Seize your opportunity in your unfavorable season for your good to become better.

What can you do to become better this season?

_____

_____

_____

_____

_____

Identify 3 triggers that prevent you from enjoying this season?

What will you do differently in this season?

_____

_____

_____

_____

_____

In a way, I was like the ants that worked hard in the summer because the winter affected their productivity to get food.

This is one of the reasons why I so enjoy living in North Carolina. I now embrace the winter months instead of dreading it. According to Thesaurus.com Winter is the cold season between autumn and spring in the northern latitudes in the Northern Hemisphere.

THE ANT

In the section above we discussed the mindset and attitude of the bear. We know that the bear hibernates during colder weather. In this section, we will learn the work ethics of the ant. "In Proverbs, chapter 6:3 "Do this now, my son, and deliver thyself, when thou art come into the hand of thy friend; go, humble thyself, and make sure thy friend. Verse 4, Give not sleep to thine eyes, nor slumber to thine eyelids. Verse 5 Deliver thyself as a roe from the hand of the Hunter, and as a bird from the hand of the Fowler. Verse 6, Go to the ant, thou sluggard: consider her ways, and be wise: Verse 7 Which having no guide, overseer, or ruler, verse 8 Provided her meat in the summer and gathered her food in the Harvest. Verse 9 How long wilt thou sleep, O sluggard? When wilt thou arise out of thy sleep"?

In this familiar passage, it is referring to the mindset, attitude, and perseverance of the ant. The ant is the smallest creature on Earth but yet, one of the hardest-working creatures. What makes the ant smarter than the bear is that when the season of summer arrives, they don't use this time as an excuse to sleep, to hang out, not to work nor relax. Instead, they go Full Speed Ahead enduring the heat and hard work while providing for their Kingdom, for providing substance for the ones that are relying on them to survive.

The ant understands it's not just about them, but their entire community. The mindset of an entrepreneur is always about others, this is why they thrive as hard as they do.

To achieve our necessary goals we must be willing to do the things that others aren't willing to do. We must be willing to get up and go to work when our bodies don't feel like it, when we don't see any productivity but yet know that this is our purpose. The ant is the wisest creature because they understand hard work. They understand that if they don't work now they won't eat later. We have adapted to an environment where we adhere to excuses and allow them to offset our lifestyle.

How many times have we said "I'll do it tomorrow" but when tomorrow comes you still have not made any effort to do what you said you were going to do. The entrepreneur has the mindset of the ant. The entrepreneur understands that much time that I put into my employment (9 to 5) I must be willing to put the same amount of hours and time into my entrepreneurship.

How can I expect to win when I don't put in enough time invested in me? The bear who knows that they cannot survive during the cold has accepted this as their fate. The ant knows that if they want to make it through the winter they must put in overtime during the warmer weather so they can come back again the following year. This is the difference between the bear and the Ant. I asked you are you a bear or are you an ant?

Do you have what it takes to be an entrepreneur?

Many people possess the great attributes and characteristics of being entrepreneurs. But do you have the muscles to be an entrepreneur? Do you have the mindset to keep going when the going gets harder or will you slip back into your hibernation season? Too many times we lose ourselves in the hustle and bustle of life. We are no strangers to putting our dreams on the shelf and convincing ourselves that this is a waste of time to pursue.

If we're not careful before you know it, twenty years have gone by and you are no further ahead in your life. The reward will be the scars of life and working a job that you are not satisfied with just to provide for your family and to pay your bills. I am here to encourage you all, who read this book, who are coachable and teachable, to shed light on the entrepreneurial spirit that lives within you.

Another great thing I am reminded of what Jim Rohn shared is to become, Wiser, Stronger, and Better. We have already discussed becoming better in your unfavorable season (time) of your life. Let's discuss becoming stronger. And how you do this is just by developing your muscles (tolerance) of overcoming difficult seasons of your life.

The ant is the wiser of the bear because of their muscle. They developed healthy work ethics to help them survive in their difficult (unfavorable seasons). The bear sleeps and the ant enjoys the fruit of their labor.

The ant becomes relentless (the entrepreneur) during this season and the bear (non-entrepreneur) complains and makes excuses.

Entrepreneurs build where the non-entrepreneurs make excuses.

This is the season to develop your entrepreneurial muscle, not give up muscle and my future grandchildren depend on (me muscle). This is the season to make things (happen muscle). I'm going to get (better muscle) because my life (depends on it muscle).

This is the season of (inventor's muscles). Imagine if no one ever tried, or failed then the possibility of all the great technology we have today wouldn't be in existence. Think about the favorable device you possess, perhaps your cell phone, iPad, or computer. What would you do if these things were never invented?

Evolution is evidence of a continued growing environment on earth. Think of the creation of the world and how magnificently God took nothing and made it into something. Again, our total existence comes from someone thinking of ideas and making it surreal.

Every entrepreneur builds their empire and legacy from an idea, thought within their imagination. Entrepreneurs make things happen while non-entrepreneurs work to make other entrepreneurs' dreams come to life and make millions and billions of dollars. My question to you is, are you an entrepreneur who makes things happen? Or are you the employee of an entrepreneur who is making his dreams and vision happen?

When you dream big you go far when you don't dream at all you wither away.

What I noticed in many people today is that it's easier to give in to your weaknesses than to pursue your vision and dreams. The difference between the bear and the ant is that the ant is Relentless. The ant knows that if they do not work harder in the warmer weather they will surely die in the cold weather. The bear chooses to hibernate to stay alive rather than finding a way to survive in the colder months.

Non-entrepreneurs are like bears. They choose to give in to excuses rather than to persevere. It's easy to say I can't, or I don't know how to then go out and face the hard work, the obstacles that were placed before them, and meet the challenges. We choose to relax and have a man-made pity party.

How many times have we heard someone say; I could have, I would have, I should have. We all know someone that tells the stories how they could have been, but they would have been having it not been for X, Y, and Z and what they should have been or what they should have done in their life. Defeat has seemed to become the new normal in our today's society. Today we have an era of Millennials who refuse to be tied down to a traditional job. We have Millennials that are sick and tired of being sick and tired of living paycheck-to-paycheck and still unable to meet their needs.

If we can learn anything from the Millennials today I hope it is to become Relentless in your thought process, Relentless in your Ambitions. Relentless in your mindset that I refuse not to live up to my full potential. I refuse to settle for mediocre. I refuse not to leave an inheritance to my children's children according to Proverbs 13: 22.

In the upcoming chapters, we're going to help you to recognize the entrepreneurial gifts that you possess within yourself. These gifts can bring you a great reward if you only have the faith to endure the right now season. The right now season is when you prepare and build. It's the season after you've written the book, and is now getting your product in the eyes of all who can and will benefit from what you have written. The right now season is being confident in you and your work whether you sold over a thousand copies of your book or none.

Ask yourself, who told you; you cannot have your own business? Ask yourself why have you not stepped into your natural-born given talents? Now ask yourself are you willing to do whatever is necessary to accomplish financial wealth success and freedom? I don't know about you but for me, I was tired of being tired. I was the one trying to make a dollar out of fifteen cents and I was fifteen cents short. I know you may be saying what does that mean? It means I had bright ideas with no money. And because of the lack of money I gave into the lifestyle that wasn't designed for me to live. I allowed the mindset of not having enough money to keep me from trying.

This is why I am writing this book to help people like you and others to tap into your Natural Born given talents and engulf yourself in the entrepreneurial lifestyle that will allow you to live the life that you were intended to live.

Are you a bear or are you an ant? We know that the bear is one of the dangerous animals that walk the Earth and can destroy you with no effort at all. But even the bear has a weak spot. And his weakness is not being able to survive in the cold seasons. I come to tell you that in your cold season is not the time to relax. It is time to become relentless. It is the time to release your inner inhibition with energy and take off and work twice as hard if not harder so you can secure your future.

We have too many people taking time off in the coldest season then we do in the warmer season. If you want to be relentless like the ant then you must be willing to do whatever it takes to survive and prepare for the coldest seasons in your life.

Use the section below to write down your goals for this season (phase of your life). Be sure to check off each item and reward yourself when accomplished.

Create a goal sheet for this section

Create a daily/weekly/monthly plan of how to accomplish your goals

Daily Weekly Monthly

SPRING

"The Rebirth of the entrepreneur in you"

Psalm 18:33 (NIV)

**"He makes my feet like the feet of a deer;
he causes me to stand on the heights."**

In this chapter, we are going to discuss our second season which is spring. Now spring and Autumn usually get confused with one another even though there's only four-season these two are very different from each other. Spring is usually associated with re-birth since the winter months have finally finished and every-thing, plant life; animal and human life is slowly getting out of its Slumber and back into the bright sunlight and tolerable weather.

I'm going to share with you a couple of words and definitions associated with the season spring from wikipedia.com. Just to give you some nouns for the word spring; jump, skip bounce, flexibility, and elasticity. The first definition is to rise, leap, move or act suddenly and swiftly, as by a sudden dark or thrust forward or outward, or being suddenly released from a coiled or con-strained position; to spring into the air, a tiger about to Spring.

This season in your life represents movement

This is the season which is very crucial to every entrepreneur and aspiring entrepreneurs to spring forth with enthusiasm. This is the season where you are being reborn or re-introduced to the entrepreneur within you.

This is when you are either releasing or creating great ideas. You are now writing down your vision and goals and checking off each item. You are moving accordingly to assure that you are on the right path of success.

You are discovering the rebirth of the hidden things you allow to be dormant in your winter seasons. The passion you once had for music, cooking, dancing, whatever it may be, the time is now to reignite the fire you let burn out. This is not the season to become complacent and lackadaisical but to move full speed ahead. Take this opportunity to advance in your newfound career path.

There's joy in spring, there's peace in spring. Even though this is the season of opportunity, you are not guaranteed to blossom. To sprout, to grow, and receive a harvest. There's no guarantee but you can take advantage of this season to further your success. Don't become distracted by the beautiful weather and now you've lost focus. This is the time to leap into action (put your business plan to use, work ethics). You must be willing to put your hands to the plow and take advantage of every free seminar/workshops, webinars, videos, and books.

You must be willing to put hard work and sweat into your passion, even if it means investing in your purpose. You must be willing to do the work even when the drought in your life is raging. When it appears that you can go no further, re visit your vision board, your goals, and dreams. Study your material and prepare yourself for the harvest.

With this revolving season, you must move with haste because this season doesn't last too long. In the book of Romans 12:11, "Not slothful in business, fervent in Spirit, and serving The LORD". Slothfulness is not welcome in spring. You only have a small window that you must gladly be willing to conquer as the passage states.

Do you recall me saying that excuses will not be accepted in this season? You must be willing to postpone or do away with anything that's not pushing you into your God's purpose in life. This isn't the time to buy a new car if you have an opportunity to open your own business. This isn't the time to be going on a shopping spree when there's a course being offered for you to receive certification.

In other words, this isn't the time to be half in and half out. Either you are all the way in or you are all the way out. Time out for being a double-minded man who is unstable in all his ways. There's another passage about not serving two masters. Either you are to love one and hate the other. This is the time in your life that either you are going to pursue your dreams and commit yourself to doing such or you will always be dreaming.

Prioritize your time so you can always be ready and available to go forth. You only have a small window of opportunity in the springtime. Don't miss yours. Life is short and no one knows the day or hours when their time is up. So until death, you must seize your moment and take advantage of every spring season you are blessed to have. Don't miss your moment.

You must seize this opportunity from the fruits of your labor.

This is the season when the rubber meets the road. The strength you have developed will now be put to use during this season. We call this season the rebirth of "you". Everything about you has been reborn again from your language, style, attitude, perseverance, your ability to achieve greatness. Your mindset and your enthusiasm for success. This is the time where no more excuses will be accepted and tolerated.

You are now well developed and equipped to handle unseen situations and will adjust accordingly. No longer will you second guess yourself but now will spring into action. You will no longer be afraid of failure and will embrace it and grow from it.

What is your desire in this season? How do I get exposure, how do I go forth in this season without breaking my pocket? These are all valid concerns and questions for every beginner entrepreneur. There are lots of ways to gain investors and even financial support to help you begin your new quest.

As a new writer, I began researching the cost to self-publish my book. The cost was astronomical. I immediately asked friends and family to assist me. This was a bad idea. I then proceeded to borrow from my retirement fund and was given over five thousand dollars to fund the cost of publishing.

Don't put yourself in a box because you don't have help from the ones you love. I admit I was discouraged when no one was willing to help me with my dreams. The key being 'My Dream". It was my responsibility to find a way to spring forth and the silence of my loved ones forced me to leap into action.

I was able to find a solution to my financial obligations. This is a great example of utilizing your employment to help fund your entrepreneurial gifts. Whatever your gifts are, begin researching ways to fund your passion.

I was determined to not let my dream of being an author die again due to the lack of financial support. Instead, I embraced the challenge of finding the means to finance my book. Don't allow the silence and the word "No" detour and discourage you from the path that you are on. If you don't believe in you, then how do you expect others to believe in you?

Many of you have had dreams since childhood that won't seem to let you go and now you are at the point that it's nagging you, it's consuming you and you got to do something about it. I encourage you to write down everything you desire to do and then make a plan. Then take the steps to execute each goal each step, day by day.

Every day you should be working towards your goals. I know you don't have time, I know you're busy; I know that you have kids and a family. Are you aware that your children's children are depending on you to leave an inheritance for them? Do you know that if you die right now your purpose dies with you, and the great gifts and talents that God has so freely given to you but never been manifested and no one would know how great thou art because you never got started?

Do you recall when you were young and vibrant and you first started in this thing called life and you said I'm just going to work this job for 10 years and then I'll branch out and do my own thing? Whether it's starting your own business, freelancing on the side whatever your passion was. And now as you look throughout the years it's 20, 30, 40 years later and you are still no further from when you first began. How do you feel?

Are you living up to your dreams? Yes or No?

What is your plan to accomplish your goals and vision?

(Write down your goals and vision)

CHAPTER 2: DEVELOPING THE ENTREPRENEUR IN YOU. RECOGNIZING WHO YOU ARE IN THE ENTREPRENEURIAL REALM

According to Thesaurus.com, the definition of an entrepreneur is; a person who organizes and manages any enterprise, especially a business, usually with considerable initiative and risk.

Many people aren't comfortable with risk and rejection. This is why it's crucial that you identify within yourself the importance of becoming an entrepreneur.

Why do you want to be an entrepreneur? Then ask yourself, do you have what it takes to be a successful entrepreneur? Can you handle adversity professionally?

Ask yourself is this you? Then ask yourself are you willing to do whatever it takes, including risk and conflict to accomplish the role and position as an entrepreneur.

The sole purpose of becoming an entrepreneur is to create passive income. Please keep in mind that many people are unaware of the terminology of passive income.

Allow me to share with you the two types of income which are; active and passive

Active income is when you work a job to earn income.

Passive income is when you create opportunities to obtain wealth.

I understand that we have been taught since day one to graduate from high school and then go to college and earn a degree and then start the journey of your career path for 20 years plus and then retire.

I know many are probably thinking, what's wrong with this scenario? Well, the problem is, while you are working to build someone else's dream; they are becoming wealthier, while you are being burned out. Ask yourself do you have the ability to live like the rich and famous and move the way they do or do you need permission from your boss to take time off and travel and enjoy your family? Please understand that there isn't anything wrong with working a traditional job. I encourage you to use your job as leverage to help push and finance your entrepreneurial lifestyle.

Many people are unaware of residual income; due to the fact of active income. According to the I.R.S., they encourage every American to have a home-based business. The reason for this is because it allows you to write off your lifestyle and take advantage of the tax breaks that you are now entitled to as a business owner and live like the wealthy.

Keep in mind there are 2 types of people, the working class and the wealthy.

The working class will work to retire and the wealthy will invest and create wealth and retire in their earlier years rather than the later years.

I recall after leaving my husband who is now my ex-husband I had no plan for my life. I felt like the children of Israel who were in the wilderness for 40 years. I had no plan, no goals, no ambition, and no sense of direction. I was alone and Clueless. I didn't know at the time that if I would have simply spent time figuring out what it was I wanted from life, I would have saved myself a lot of heartache, pain, and disappointment.

Because I failed to plan I fell on my face so many times that if I had a dollar for every failure and disappointment I would have been a millionaire a long time ago.

My first entrepreneurial experience is when I was homeless in 1994. I had no money, no income and to top it off I was pregnant with daughter number four. I was unable to seek employment due to my toxic pregnancy. I had less than $100 to my name and all I knew was that I had three children that I needed to provide for.

I didn't know what it was then but I know now that it was the voice of the Holy Spirit talking to me and leading me. The Voice told me to use my gifts and trust God. The gifts that I knew at the time that would bring me instant results and cash was cooking. So I went with the shelter director of activities in the van and went to the grocery store and I began to purchase the items needed to make sweet potato pies, lasagna, baked macaroni and cheese, and fried chicken.

I didn't set out on a mission to raise money and to become an entrepreneur. My sole purpose was to provide for my children and our needs right now. Imagine if I would have stayed on course with my entrepreneurial gifts. I could have, I would have saved myself more time, less heartache, and disappointment. This is the beginning of a spiraling rendition of the children of Israel, who were to have a 3-day journey, which turned into 40 years. This was the story of my life. It'll take me over forty years to finally be doing what God has purposed for me to do.

In the book of Hosea chapter 4: 6, "it says my people are destroyed for lack of knowledge; because thou Hast rejected knowledge, I will also reject thee, that thou should be no priest to me; since thou hast forgotten the law of thy God, I will also forget thy Children."

I come to tell you it is better late than never to activate your faith and produce the abilities of your God-given natural talent and leave an impact on the world. See I was an entrepreneur when I was homeless but I just didn't know it. Imagine if I would have continued on that path I'm almost confident that it would have brought me millions of dollars because that's how great I am with my talents, that God has given me.

If I was making money and it helped me to obtain a certain goal why would I not continue? Fear crept in and told me that I did not have enough money or, I don't have what it takes to start my own business. And guess what, I listened. I obliged my fear and went down a long treacherous mountainous Road that almost left me destitute.

Who said I couldn't start a business with no money? The problem is that we think too much about things that have no concern to us. It would have been easier had I continued baking my pies and giving them away as gifts to family and friends. This would have allotted me the opportunity to market my pies and build clientele.

Had I continued on this journey, I would have discovered the necessary steps to pursue my career in baking/catering? The first step is getting my certification for food handling. The next step knows the laws and requirements in whatever state you live in to get your kitchen inspected to be certified to prepare and sell foods and of course whatever business license you may need. All of these steps are doable on an economical budget.

List five business goals to accomplish this year?

Now list the steps you are prepared to take to accomplish these five steps

What if I told you that there was a way for you to make money doing the things that you love? Will this ignite the entrepreneur inside of you? Would you feel that now is the opportunity for you to Branch out and do the things that you love and which you have shunned from this idea? The truth is that it's okay to be afraid. After all, you're doing something that you've never done before; especially in an open forum.

As you begin to take your passion from imagination to life, it's the season to continually build. Take the initiative to begin advertising your new-found love such as creating business cards and flyers. Set up your business pages on social media such as Facebook, Instagram, and Twitter and other platforms that offer these free services.

It's time for the bear in you to awaken and arise. it's time for you to go Full Speed Ahead without looking back. Are you ready?

Personal Development

Now that the entrepreneur in you has awakened, it is now time for you to take the proper steps to assure you will not result back to familiar behaviors. To have success, you must first change your mindset and unhealthy habits that have detained your grand appearance to the entrepreneurial realm.

What are you listening to each day that will help you accomplish your goals? What can help feed and form your ideas into an empire?

If you are listening to a bunch of nonsense that is not going to help you in your personal development and growth then you are behind. I'm reminded of my husband who always tells me I need to watch things that are going to feed my spiritual man. If you are anything like me ladies, I enjoy reality television shows. I love watching the Housewives of Atlanta and Married to Medicine. I'm not saying that there's anything wrong with this, but keep in mind that these ladies are already established. No matter what foolishness they display on television every one of these women in their rightful place is already entrepreneurial bosses.

Did you pay attention to every one of them has multiple streams of cash flow coming into their household whether it's cosmetic lines, t-shirts, and hair bundles; whatever it is they are doing it to the utmost. What about you? What can you gain by watching these types of shows?

Are you spending more time with things that are feeding your ambitions or are you spending more time with things that are preventing you from prevailing?

If you want to be relentless, you must be willing to do the things that you have never done before. That means giving up things that prevented you from once doing that now are comfortable doing on a daily basis. All the successful people I know, all the wealthy people I know get up when everyone else is sleeping. Eric Thomas says "I get up at 3 a.m. in the morning because I'm relentless."

What are you willing to do to accomplish your dreams? Write a list of things that you are willing to do on a daily basis that will help recondition your mindset and help you accomplish your dreams.

In this season it is now your time leap into action and to fulfill your God-given purpose. It is your duty to get everything that your heart desires if you only believe. Time is on your side during this season. You now have more day time savings then you would have in the colder seasons. I like to say I rather work hard now and play harder later. Catch this revelation and apply it to your life.

What are you thinking?

Developing healthy habits and daily routines.

In the 23rd chapter of proverbs verse 7 it reads as follows "as he thinketh in his heart, so is he; eat and drink, saith he to thee; but his heart is not with thee. "

In this familiar Passage, it is explaining we are what we think. If you think highly of yourself, you will always excel and if you think poorly of yourself, then you will always underachieve and second guess yourself. We must fuel ourselves with positive energy and thoughts.

We are now in the season of the year of the underdog. This is the time that people are springing into action. No longer are people wasting valuable time talking about what they desire to do. Many have taken advantage of becoming wiser, stronger, and better. I'm reminded of a quote from an unknown author, "Time will pass, will you?" Again I ask you how you begin your day? How you begin your day is how you will live your life. If you begin with no plan, you have failed to plan your day let alone week month or year is a strong indicator your life is going to be in disarray.

I am a strong believer that as you begin your day with healthy exercises and routines on a daily basis that it will all pay off after a while. I begin each day giving God thanks, praise, and glory for all he has done for me. I am reminded of an inspirational video from Mr. Steve Harvey himself and he said before he asked God for anything he thanked him, for all his blessings, health, and family first.

My husband and I not only agree with this we have adapted to this same mindset before we ask God for anything, we acknowledge him, but we also thank him and we glorify him. So we begin each day with a prayer thanking God. Next, we recite our daily affirmations that we agree and believe it to be so for our lives. Then we read the word of God together. We read scriptures that are encouraging us to stand and to grow. And after, we ask the things our heart desires. Then we listen to motivational videos of great speakers, such as; Steve Harvey, Jim Rohn, Grant Cardone, Joel Olsteen, Les Brown. We find a motivational speaker to speak and share wisdom as they bestow knowledge unto us as we gravitate to their successes and nuggets they willingly give unto us.

The importance of how you begin your day will eventually mirror your entire life. You are now in a position where you could go from the bottom to the top, It all depends on how you are, and how you reprogram your mind to go forward and not backward. In the word of God, it says "I'm forgetting the things that are behind me, and I'm pressing towards the things that are before me."

In this season it's time for you to bounce back so you can get back to your first true love. Allow me to be the first to congratulate you because today is the first day, of the best day, of the rest of your life. As we close out this chapter if you have not done so already, and even if you have already done so maybe it's time for you to reevaluate how you begin your day.

Take this opportunity to create a daily routine that can help mold and lead you In the direction of success.

SUMMER

Matthew 24:45 King James Version (KJV)

"Who then is a faithful and wise servant, whom his lord hath made ruler over his household, to give them meat in due season?"

The next season that we are going to talk about is the hottest season of the year. This is also another short season; which occurs in the months of June until September. Many confuse this season to take time off from hard work and relax. This is the most crucial period of your life.

CHAPTER 3: CULTIVATING AND NOURISHING YOUR VALUES

The hard work you've begun in the first two seasons of your life now needs to be nourished and protected. This is not the season to become complacent and enjoy the good weather. Every idea, vision, and goals you have designed for yourself must be guarded against fear, comfortability, slothfulness. Remember the ant is relentless in this season.

You must begin to fuel your inner man by studying more, looking for locations, investors, and answers and solutions. You must be steadfast and unmovable. Fear can only take refuge if you are not moving.

This is the season when you must defend yourself against the enemy. "Your Enemies "The two things we meet in this season are opportunities and challenges. This is your season to grow as you have never grown before but watch out for the enemy that has enabled you for many seasons.

Imagine once you have planted your seeds, crops in your garden but now you must protect it from insects, pesticides, animals. Everything and anything that can and will prevent it from growing (prospering). You set out on a mission to protect your harvest by fighting off the uninviting enemies that will kill your seed.

You must be willing to do the same thing with the gifts you possess. The entrepreneur in you is waiting to bud, but you must be equipped and strong enough to stay away from your deadly and silent killer.

You must stay out of the end zones. The zones that will have you going backward instead of forward if you are not careful. Stay away from these zones:

- Safe zone
- Familiar zone
- It's the too hard zone
- Comfort zone
- Lazy zone
- I give up zone
- Lucky zone
- Lonely zone

The safe zone will have you giving just the bare minimum to stay relevant. I equate this zone with paying just the bare minimum to keep your credit cards activated. Even though you followed the regulations, there's a high penalty cost that is attached to the bare minimum and this is the interest rate sky-rocketing.

In this season you must be willing to nourish and protect your ideas, dreams, and vision. Do not get comfortable in this zone because it's safe. Begin launching your ideas. Take it from the vision board and now put a plan in action. Inquire information of how to go from step one to completion.

The next zone is the "familiar zone'. This is usually when you are familiar with a certain scenario, place or this is your territory. This is when we usually become cocky and take this zone for granted. This is not the right attitude to have in this zone. Seize this opportunity to learn something new and apply it while you're in this zone.

Do not take this zone for granted. This zone could be your enemy if you do not recognize what you need to be doing... It's very easy to get stuck here if you are not careful.

The next zone is your "Comfort Zone". This zone is similar to your familiar zone. Again this is the zone when people often miss their window of opportunity due to giving just enough to stay afloat. I equate this zone with a person working a job for over 20 years. They complain daily how much they despise it. And when you ask the question, "how come you won't leave and go someplace else or start your own business"? It's always the same answer, I don't want to start over, or I'm familiar here. So the person manages to do just enough, not to get fired.

In this zone, you need to give 120 percent instead of 25 percent. This is the zone when getting up at 5 am, when everyone else is asleep gives you the leverage of your day. And with discipline and consistency, your day will turn into weeks, months, and finally years. This is the advantage you will need to go against your enemies which are the competitors.

The next zone is the "Lazy Zone" and this is the zone you will want to avoid at all costs necessary. This is the place that you will feel entitled to do nothing. The justification being you've worked all year and now you want to relax. Warning, caution ahead. This isn't the right mindset if you have not accomplished what you set out to do originally.

Ask yourself, have you done the work necessary to enjoy this time off? You will find the ant working harder in this season to guarantee they have the necessities for the colder months. Avoid this zone by any means necessary. Protect your vision and continue working. The time will come when you will enjoy the fruit of your labor.

Another zone I urge you to avoid is the "I give up zone". This is the zone usually when you're right at the edge of the finished product, but unable to see the results. This is the zone where you usually have a pity party with yourself. This is the zone where you feel alone and doesn't have the support of the ones you are closest to such as family and friends. This is the zone that you convince yourself that you don't deserve greatness and convince yourself to quit. Do not allow yourself to become distracted from what you do not see or have. Focus on your breakthrough and completing your assignment.

The next zone is the "Lucky Zone". This is the zone where no effort is necessary. You don't have to produce hard work to improve and master your gifts. This is the place because you're a great singer; you can pull it off based on your luck and skill and still do a good job. The only problem is that you will never truly know your full potential until you challenge yourself. This is the zone that nothing is required of you and you are okay with it.

This is where you begin to lose greatness of your talent because you didn't protect, nourish, enhance, and cherish it. This is where your gifts die off in the lucky zone. I don't need to practice, I'm already good. This may be true but you will never begin to monetize the full value when you settle for mediocre.

All of these challenges are a major part of the summertime, which means the season for you to protect, value and nourish. If not careful you can get stuck in this season and wither away.

You cannot fight the enemy with your power. You are not skilled, experienced, and equipped for the battle. You must begin to prepare for war. I know you're probably thinking, "what war"? The war that will prevent you from living the life you were intended to live. You must study and advance your skills to succeed.

I love singing and in fact, I believe I am up there with Barbara Streisand, Celine Dion, Mary J. Blige, and Beyonce. My gift is a blessing. However, for me to advance in my craft, it must be perfected. I must enhance my skills by taking vocal lessons and then utilizing what I learn throughout the day. I must work on breathing techniques, walking, talking, learning my notes, and going over everything I've learned until I master it. This isn't the time for me to be in the end zones of life.

Cultivating the entrepreneur in you;

Quote: "Dreams without goals are just dreams and they ultimately fuel disappointment'- Denzel Washington

I'm reminded of something that Denzel Washington has spoken and he said: "True desire in the heart, for anything good, is God's proof to you sent beforehand to indicate that it's yours already". I interpreted this as whatever my passion is, writing, cooking, singing, the proof is already within me.

You are an entrepreneur before you even know the meaning of the word. You were born to be an entrepreneur. We usually find out or realize it when we give our gifts to bless others without capitalizing on it. For instance, if you are a baker, how many times have you baked for the love of it and blessed family, friends, neighbors, and co-workers for the fulfillment of your passion? Perhaps sewing is your talent, and you make scarves, hats, and blankets and give them away for special occasions and holidays?

This is proof that God has sent to you as evidence that he has created you to be more than just an employee. This is the season that you seize the opportunity to go forth in your true heart desires.

I believe when you do it to help encourage and (empower others) then God will take care of you. The sole purpose for wanting to do this particular book is so that I can help prevent many from making the same mistakes I've made.

God has given me these great talents to use for good, so I use them to help fuel others that if I can do it, a girl from Wyandanch, NY, no money, mother of five children. If I can do it, then so can you.

The key is you must be consistent in your work ethics. Don't take anything for granted. Even if you are excelling, don't take it for granted. Seize the moment to help someone else grasp the concept. Reach one, teach one is something we are all familiar with.

Another essential key is just don't aspire to make a living. Aspire to make a difference. Commit yourself to the spirit of excellence. Commit to becoming better. A better you, wife, husband, parent, child, boss, entrepreneur. You owe it to yourself to be the best you. Give your best and nothing less.

It's important to know that failure is a part of success. "Your Success". Embrace your failures and shortcomings and learn from them. Use them to help enhance your strengths. It's okay to fall but learn how to fall forward. When life knocks you down, instead of falling flat on your face, reposition yourself to see where you are landing.

Life is so much better when you have a set destination, and with destination comes directions. When going from point A to point B. There must be a set location you desire to reach. And to reach your destination, you will need specific directions to arrive. You need directions to achieve your entrepreneurial destinations and the directions you will need are goals. Specific goals.

Dreams without goals are just dreams. It's not that there isn't enough time in the day, it's everything to do with not knowing how to prioritize your time wisely and setting specific goals. What you learn to master today will allow you to live financially free for the rest of your life. But you must be willing to do the work now, in this season, no matter how difficult and challenging it may be.

My first book was full of errors and I paid two editors great money to assure me this would not happen. Needless to say, when the books arrived, I cried. I cried because as a professional, this wasn't a good look for me.

In the beginning, I was refusing to sell my books, and believe me I was very adamant about this. My husband, on the other hand, was looking at the business side of this. We had spent close to 5,000 dollars and he was interested in making our money back and including a profit.

He went on to sell to anyone and everyone including my co-workers who were all teachers. You can imagine the anguish I was experiencing. I decided to inform everyone about the errors, so I didn't have to face the criticism after all failure doesn't feel good. Right? Wrong! I was so far from the mark because of fear of failure I was taking away from the content. My colleagues embraced me and supported me in all my endeavors in writing.

Have there never been any errors, I would not know the things I know today that has made me a better writer and publisher. I had to embrace my mistakes to grow. What intrigued me is that a stranger, who I didn't know encouraged me and told me to concentrate on the content and not the errors. Is it a good book they asked? Yes, I replied. Does it have a strong message and solution, they asked? Yes. Then many will overlook the mistakes and concentrate on the storyline.

I am honored to say that today, many women still ask me to come to speak at their events due to my first book "A Mother's Time to Heal". I almost missed my opportunity because of a few mistakes. I fell forward and continued writing (and yes still some mistakes) but with each book, I became better, wiser and it reflects in my writing.

Use this opportunity to revisit what your passions are and seize the opportunity to go forth.

FALL

Genesis 2:1&2 King James Version (KJV)

1 Thus the heavens and the earth were finished and all the host of them.

2 And on the seventh day, God ended his work which he had made; and he rested on the seventh day from all his work which he had made.

This is the final season and you will find that it takes place in the months of September until the middle of December. In this season it's not too hot and not too cold. This is the season where everything comes together. It's like a full circle. Don't confuse the leaves falling from the trees that you have lost. This season is just the opposite of losing. This is your winning season. This is the time of your life that the manifestation of all your hard work will surely pay off. Your concepts and ideas are thoroughly organized into a perfect business plan for your business. You have developed healthy daily habits and routines; you have done the groundwork and now it's time to watch it all come together. Fall is the season of completion.

This is when you will experience the full manifestation of what you have been preparing for your entire life.

CHAPTER 4: FALLING INTO PLACE

"For where your treasure is, there will your heart be also."
Luke 12:34

This is the part of your life when you have taken on the mindset and lifestyle of the "Spirit of Excellence". This is when you will now begin doing things decently and in order. No more slacking and sabotaging your true worth. You understand that whatever your heart desires are, that God will give to you.

This is the time that everything you have worked hard for in the other seasons (through the year) is now coming to pass. You get to not only see the fruit of your labor but enjoy them as well. This is the result of your commitments, excellence, and your thorough and specific planning and your ability to focus.

This is the time in your life that your gifts will bring you in the presence of great men. "A Man's gift maketh room for him, and bringeth him before great men". Proverbs 18:16. People will come from all over to learn and see your greatness and contribution to the world.

You have heeded to the passage in the book of Romans 12:11 where it says, "Not slothful in business; fervent in Spirit and Serving The LORD". Your newfound concept and love to have discipline and financial freedom has outweighed your slothfulness and now have you at the top of your game.

No more procrastinating when there is so much more you can be doing with your time and your life. You are now doing things intentionally and deliberately. Everything is well thought out and planned accordingly before taking action.

You have learned how to concentrate on the things at hand instead of running away from the challenges. You now have answers for solutions then pretending. You have learned how to weather the storms of your life and you no longer hibernate when the going gets tough.

Recognizing Your Strengths

Ever since I was a little girl I had great admiration for music and literature. I love singing, reading, and writing. Even though I enjoyed singing and writing; there was something that prevented me from going forth. The first thing was or is, I cannot dance. I have no coordination whatsoever. And the second thing is, even though I can write a good book, a great storyline, I am horrific with editing.

These two simple things were a major roadblock for me almost my entire life. Due to inconsistency and slothfulness, not only did I miss out on major opportunities, but I also yielded to my stumbling blocks and because of disobedience, I've reaped what I've sown.

I was focusing on not having all the pieces of the puzzle to be a successful songstress and writer that I missed out on possibly being one of the greatest in these genres.

Begin spending more time on your natural strengths instead of focusing on what you do not have. I can now tell you that I have built my businesses around my natural gifts and strengths.

As a writer, I have a phenomenal team that assures the quality of my work. Before this book goes through the final phases of publication, it will go through the process of being edited, refined, and fine-tuned. You will never get to see what it looks like before printing.

Just like the beautiful diamonds we all love and wear. Before the pretty sparkling and shininess, the diamond is a small black, ugly object. It must go through the refining process, before being made into the many beautiful images we see and purchase. The same for our nice vehicles we drive daily. Before put together, it's pieces of metal.

This is the season of your life when you take nothing out of something and create something great. And something great is your entrepreneurial business.

In this phase of your life, fear and inconsistency should not be present. If there's anything perhaps still lurking around from the old you, then it must be destroyed immediately. Go back to the drawing board if necessary. Rearrange goals, visions, and time-lines if necessary, but whatever you do, "Don't Stop". Ask your-self, are you getting everything you are entitled to? Did you do the hard work, regardless of any obstacles that were placed in your path? Are you an overcomer? Above all are you a bear or an ant?

If you have done everything that is required of you, then the only thing left to do is watch your master building come to pass. Your hard work, prayers, and consistency are paying off in this phase of your life. Reward yourself for not giving up nor making excuses.

When your business starts to fall into place you will identify the 5 C's of having success in business. Let me start with Communication. Communication is a major key to success in business and life. You will either have to communicate with business partners, vendors, employees, customers and the list go on and on. If you elect to have a home-based or online business your communication is limited to emails, facetime, chats, blogs, and some phone interactions. Lack of communication can be the downfall for many in their businesses.

My favorite C of the 5 is Commitment. Commitment is one of the most important of them all. Without commitment, you have no structure, no discipline, no order, or foundation. When there is no commitment there is no heartbeat for the vision of the business. Commitment requires drive and encouragement.

The 3rd C is Consistency. The major problem for most business owners is the lack of consistency. Most are being consistent at being inconsistent. In business your income, money, volume, stock, revenue all are based upon you being consistent working your business, sharing and showing your business, and or working your network. Entrepreneurs always have to work their business 24/7. They have to be consistent in marketing, advertising, promotions, and networking your business.

The 4th C is Common Sense. I know this one is tough, however, it is needed and necessary to have success in business.

Common Sense is not common, but when making decisions you have to ask yourself "do this make sense?" or "will this make money or lose money?" If the truth be told if business owners used more common sense than emotions they would be more successful.

The final C is Collaboration. This is a critical part of having a successful business. You will always need someone to bounce ideas off and get a new or another perspective. Collaborations produce the best business ideas and products and services. Please be careful who your sounding board is. Please consider getting a Mentor and or a Coach. Never think that you are the smartest one in your circle and that you know it all.

Now that you have the 5 C's of having a successful business nothing will stop you. This next section is going to bless you richly. These last several sections are bonuses from me to you.

Active Income verse Passive Income

Here are 3 sole purposes of passive income vs active income:

- Identify what your benchmark/ bookmark is
- What are the gaps that are preventing you from reaching your benchmarks?
- Your future is in your daily routine

The bear becomes lazy and inferior in its off season and the ant dominates and becomes superior in its offseason

Quote: *"A Bend in the road is not the end of the road. Unless you fail to make the turn"*- Unknown

I know you're probably saying is when will my big break or moment come.

Here are a few nuggets to help you:

1. Work while you wait
2. Work on your focus (perspective is everything)you see difficult as negative
3. Work on your faith- recite scripture
4. Work on yourself
5. Important things: Setting goals that will help take you from dreaming to now doing.
6. Set power goals to help enhance your vision. Break these goals into 3 categories: Specific goals, Measurable goals, and put a time limit on your goal.
7. A specific goal must be precise. For example: To say you want to grow your business isn't precise. To say, "My goal is to increase my business by adding new business partners". You've now specified your intent to grow your business.

8. A measurable goal is, " My goal is to increase my business by adding new business partners of 50 percent, Just by adding the 50 percent you've measured your goals.

9. Adding a time limit to your goal makes you accountable. My goal is to increase my business by adding new business partners by 50 percent by December 21, 2020.

10. Keep in mind many people are only familiar with active income (employment)

11. To create generational wealth you must transition from active income to passive income.

12. You need passive income. Must put yourself in a position to do something serious that you'll be paid from it forever in the form of residual income.

13. How much is your freedom worth?

What are the Four Seasons of Your Life?

Yearly Goal Sheet

Today I Accomplished:

Date:

BUSINESS OPPORTUNITIES

MyEcon $29.95 to start and only $34.95 a month to maintain

www.6figureswithadolph.com

Easy1up

https://easy1up.com/?id=adolphmoore

This is an International Business Opportunity that is still a home-based business. Click Join Now on the page to get started...

Abundance Network

https://salesrobot.ai/ava/?ref=adolphmoore

www.mailboxcash123.com

Or Call Ava the robot for info 386-518-0304

This an automated system where you can total work from your phone with the SMS system.

Lead Lightning Affiliate

www.cashonoffline.com

FOREIGN EXCHANGE TRADING (TRADERA)

This is an International Business Opportunity in over 80 countries and is still a home-based business.

http://bit.ly/Forex_Overview

http://bit.ly/Forex_Tradera_Payplan

FACEBOOK GROUP

http://bit.ly/Forex_Cash_Fun

TO SIGN UP

www.paidnstyle.com or call (910) 514- 3448

I feel good to have accomplished my weekly goals:

_____

_____

_____

_____

_____

_____

_____

_____

_____

_____

_____

_____

_____

_____

_____

_____

_____

_____

_____

_____

_____

_____

I feel good to have accomplished my weekly goals:

_____

_____

_____

_____

_____

_____

_____

_____

_____

_____

_____

_____

_____

_____

_____

_____

_____

_____

_____

_____

_____

_____

I feel good to have accomplished my weekly goals:

_____

_____

_____

_____

_____

_____

_____

_____

_____

_____

_____

_____

_____

_____

_____

_____

_____

_____

_____

_____

_____

_____

Personal and Entrepreneurial Self-Assessment

Do you have what it takes to be an entrepreneur?

1. I like to give myself challenges when taking on new projects? True or False

2. I am fairly at ease in difficult situations? True or False

3. I find it rather difficult to wake up at 5:00 am daily? True or False

4. I enjoy getting up early in the morning to work on me? True or False?

5. I believe in setting goals I can achieve? True or False

6. I am a procrastinator and wait until the last minute to get things done? True or False

7. I am a good listener and follow sound instructions? True or False

8. I make excuses for not getting things done? True or False

9. I am fearful of rejection? True or False

10. When faced with difficulties, I look for alternative solutions? True or False

11. It's possibly easy for me to influence one's destiny? True or False

12. In general, I distrust my instincts. True or False

13. I believe in having the final say. True or False

14. I can get by on luck and skills? True or False

15. Discipline isn't necessary to be successful? True or False

16. Hard work isn't necessary to build an empire? True or False

17. I am coachable and teachable? True or False

18. I believe I have what it takes to be a leader? True or False

19. I am ambitious. True or False

20. I am determined to establish financial freedom and wealth. True or False

21. I embrace and grow from my failures. True or False

22. For me, everything is possible if I believe I can do it. True or False

23. I cannot function in stressful situations? True or False

24. I find it easy to motivate others to work with me? True or False

25. I find it difficult to make sacrifices to succeed. True or False

26. I give in easily when faced with a difficult task. True or False

27. I am an influencer. True or False

28. I take on easy tasks to make myself look good. True or False

29. I am not good at leading others. True or False

30. I have a hard time functioning in uncertain or ambiguous situations. True or False

31. I appreciate situations where there are rules to respect. True or False

32. I will not allow finances to dictate my success. True or False?

33. I always calculate opportunities based on my finances. True or False

34. I tend to put off difficult tasks until later. True or False

35. I am not afraid to take on initiatives. True or False

36. I prefer being my own boss. True or False

37. I rather work for my employer, then for myself. True or False

38. Being ambitious and energetic is often perceived poorly. True or False

39. I will always rise to the occasion. True or False

40. I believe being an entrepreneur is the freedom every human being should possess. True or False

41. I believe in having multiple streams of cash flow. True or False

42. I will commit to my entrepreneurial gifts to build financial stability and wealth. True or False

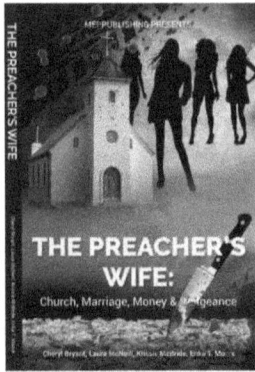

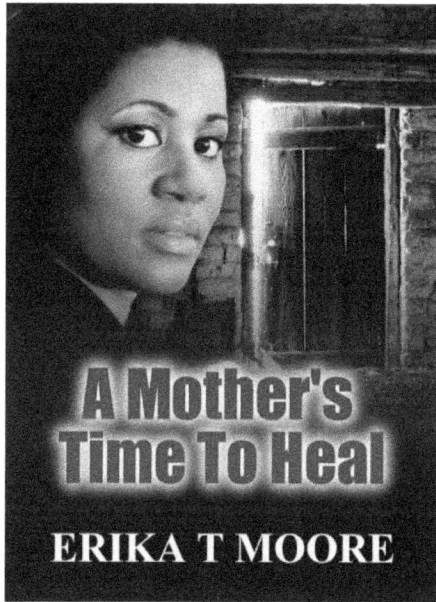

You can purchase any one of these books from

www.meppublishing.com

www.erikatmoore.com

www.adolphmoore.com